Juicing for Beginners

1000 Days Juicing Recipes to Lose Weight, Gain Energy, Fight
Disease, Detox, and Live Long.
Bonus Crash Course to Make Tasty Juice

DENISE ROGERS

Table of Contents

15. POTASSIUM PUNCH SMOOTHIE,

16. FRUIT AND SEEDS SMOOTHIE

17. SMOOTHIES MADE WITH SUMMER STONE FRUITS

18. CARROT CAKE SMOOTHIE

19. ENERGY BOOSTING SMOOTHIE

20. CREAMY AVOCADO AND KALE SMOOTHIE

21. STRAWBERRY, BANANA, AND OATMEAL SMOOTHIE

22. SMOOTHIE MADE WITH ALMONDS, BANANAS, AND FLAX SEEDS

23. SMOOTHIE MADE WITH SPINACH, MANGO, AND CARROTS TO DRINK

24. SMOOTHIE MADE WITH OATMEAL, BANANAS, AND STRAWBERRIES

25. SMOOTHIE MADE WITH PEANUT BUTTER, BANANAS, AND JELLY.

26. SMOOTHIE WITH AVOCADO AND BANANA, HIGH IN PROTEIN

27. BLUEBERRY AND COCONUT MILK SMOOTHIE MADE WITH BLUEBERRIES

28. PROTEIN SMOOTHIE MADE WITH SPINACH, BANANAS, AND FLAX

29. PUMPKIN PROTEIN SMOOTHIE WITH PUMPKIN AND GINGER

30. SMOOTHIE MADE WITH AVOCADO, SPINACH, AND KIWI

31. CHOCOLATE BERRY SMOOTHIE WITH CHOCOLATE AND BERRIES

Detoxifying and cleansing juice

32. THE MORNING ENERGIZER JUICE

33. JUICE MADE FROM CARROTS, APPLES, AND GINGER

34. HEALTHIEST AND MOST DELICIOUS GREEN JUICE

35. THE TRADITIONAL BEET JUICE

36. GOLDEN SWEET GREEN JUICE

37. HOMEMADE V8 JUICE

38. TRADITIONAL ALMOND MILK

39. GREEN BEET CLEANSE

40. VEGGIE VITAE

41. DANDELION DELIGHT

42. FENNEL AND GREENS

43. BRING SOME LIFE TO YOUR LIVER JUICE

44. COCKTAIL FOR DETOXIFICATION

45. ANTIOXIDANTS PLUS

46. ORANGE PINEAPPLE CHILI

47. DELICIOUS CARROTS WITH SPINACH.

48. JUICE PREPARED FROM BROCCOLI CHOKE

49. LEAFY GREEN DELIGHT

50. COCKTAIL MADE WITH CUCUMBERS AND CARROTS

51. GREEN BEAST

52. SPROUTS OF PEPPER

53. CLEANSE WITH CRANBERRIES AND WATERMELON

54. TEA MADE WITH WATERMELON SEEDS

55. LEMONADE

56. JUICE OF ENVY

57. CRAN BEET WATERMELON

58. LEMONADE WITH CRANBERRIES

59. SMOOTHIE MADE WITH STRAWBERRY AND BANANA.

60. SPROUT OF CELERY AND PEPPER

61. A BLAST OF BERRY AND MELON.

62. LEMONADE WITH CHERRY AND BERRY BLEND

63. CHILLED PLUM AND MELON DRINK

64. GUAVALOUPE GOODIE

65. GREEN SHIELD

Vegetable juice

66. CARROT, CUCUMBER, CELERY, AND APPLE JUICE

67. JUICE MADE FROM CARROTS, TOMATOES, AND APPLE

68. JUICE MADE WITH BROCCOLI, CARROTS, APPLES, AND BEETROOTS

69. REFRESHING BLEND OF GREEN JUICE

70. A MIXTURE OF FRESH SPINACH, APPLE, AND LEMON JUICE

Antiaging juice

71. ORANGE CARROT

72. THE DRINK OF BUGS

73. JUICE TO THE C TO SEE

74. THE PLEASURE IS ALL MINE, JUICE.

75. JUICE MADE FROM PUMPKIN

76. SWEET POTATO PIE

77. VEGGIE BOOST

78. SEEING GREEN

79. THE PLEASURE OF APRICOTS

80. GREEN POPEYE JUICE

81. PUNCH WITH PINEAPPLE AND CHERRIES

82. JULEP WITH CHERRY, BERRY, AND MINT

83. APPLE JUICE WITH MINT

84. POTATO PINEAPPLE SPLASH

85. JUICE MADE FROM POMEGRANATES AND CHERRIES

86. SIMPLY ORANGE

Juicing

Fresh fruit and or vegetables are often ground, squeezed, or pressed to extract their juice during the juicing process. The method of pressing newly picked fruits to get immediate access to the nutrients in such fruits is known by its more contemporary name, cold pressing.

Juicing originated in the 1920s and 1930s, but the 1970s were the decade in which it took off as a craze. By the 1990s, healthy eating and juice bars were becoming more commonplace among the general population.

Fresh juice is a simple method to get various nutrients, including vitamins and minerals. However, even though evidence supports juicing, the possible health benefits might vary greatly depending on the specific ingredients used to make the juice. If you aren't cautious, you could consume unhealthy calories and sugar via the beverages you drink.

Benefits of Juicing

➤ **Increased Consumption of Nutrients**

Your body can absorb nutrients more rapidly when you drink juice because it does not have to work as hard to break down fibers and the other components included in entire meals. You may acquire more vitamins and minerals by drinking juice, perhaps more than your typical diet. This is because juice contains concentrated forms of these nutrients. It's conceivable that you're not getting enough of certain nutrients if you don't eat many fresh fruits and vegetables in their complete forms.

➤ **Support for the Cardiovascular System**

consuming pure juice from fruits and vegetables may raise blood levels of nitric oxide. Your blood vessels will stay flexible and healthy thanks to the effects of nitric oxide, which include opening up your blood vessels and lowering your blood pressure.

➤ **Possible Dangers Involved with Consuming Juice**

It's possible that the potential health advantages of juicing won't be worth it in the end. These potential dangers may be increased or decreased depending on how much juice you consume, how often you consume it, and what kinds of fruits and vegetables are used to make it:

➤ **An Unhealthy Amount of Calories**

There are calories in all fruits and vegetables, but these calories are balanced out by the other components, such as fiber and other tissues. It is vital to control how much you consume of various juices since an 8-ounce glass typically contains between 100 and 180 calories. An excess of calories might cause a person to acquire weight.

➤ **Too Much Sugar Intake**

Sugar is the primary contributor to the calorie content in fruit juice. Because there is fiber in juice to slow down the body's absorption of sugar, people who drink juice often notice a jump in their blood sugar levels after drinking it. Consuming vegetable juices that are either entirely or mostly composed of vegetables is the most effective strategy to reduce the amount of sugar you take in daily.

➢ **Insufficient Amount of Fiber and Protein**

Drinking juice of any kind (including vegetable juice) may contribute to malnutrition since juice of any kind has very little fiber or protein, if any at all. This includes vegetable juice. Fiber is essential for maintaining healthy digestive function, whereas protein is important for maintaining healthy muscles, bones, and blood.

Smoothies

It is common for smoothies to be thick and creamy drinks made from a variety of puréed fruits and vegetables as well as a variety of other ingredients.
The most basic kind of smoothie calls for only two primary components: a base and some kind of liquid. From then on, you may mix and match the elements to your satisfaction.

The chilly, frosty smoothness of a milkshake is achieved in the final result by using frozen fruits and vegetables or ice cubes in several smoothie recipes. The taste profiles, on the other hand, might be quite different from one another, depending on the components.

Typical ingredients

The following are common components used in homemade smoothies as well as those purchased from stores:
➢ Berries, bananas, apples, peaches, mangoes, and pineapples are some examples of fruits.
➢ Kale, spinach, arugula, wheatgrass, microgreens, avocado, cucumber, beetroot, cauliflower, and carrots are some of the vegetables used in this dish.
➢ Almond butter, peanut butter, walnut butter, flax meal, chia seeds, hemp seeds, and sunflower seed butter are some of the nut and available seed butter.
➢ Ginger, turmeric, cinnamon, cacao powder, cacao nibs, parsley, and basil are some of the herbs and spices used.
➢ Spirulina, bee pollen, powder, protein powder, and powdered versions of vitamin and mineral supplements are some examples of nutritional and herbal supplements.
➢ Examples of liquids include water, fruit juice, vegetable juice, milk, non-dairy milk, coconut water, iced tea, and cold brew coffee.
➢ Some of the sweeteners may be used are maple syrup, raw sugar, honey, pitted dates, simple syrup, fruit juice concentrates, stevia, ice cream, and sorbet.
➢ Other options include yogurt made from dairy or non-dairy products, cottage cheese, vanilla essence, soaked oats, cooked white beans, and silken tofu.

Types

The vast majority of smoothies may be placed under either one of the following categories or both, despite the fact that there is much overlap between them:

Fruit smoothies. This particular form of smoothie often consists of one or more kinds of fruit mixed with fruit juice, water, milk, or ice cream.

Smoothies made with greens. Blended with water, fruit juice, or milk, green smoothies include a variety of leafy green vegetables as well as fruit. Although they sometimes include a small amount of fruit for flavor, they typically include a greater proportion of vegetables than ordinary smoothies.

Smoothies made with protein. The foundation of a protein smoothie is often made up of one fruit or vegetable, a beverage, and a significant quantity of protein-rich ingredients such as protein powder, Greek yogurt, cottage cheese, or silken tofu.

Benefits

➢ Consumption of Fruits and Vegetables Should be Raised

Smoothies have the distinct advantage of being able to conceal the presence of practically any fruit and a significant number of vegetables without compromising their overall appeal or flavor. According to several studies, consuming an adequate amount of fruits and vegetables daily reduces one's risk of developing chronic. However, the recommended daily consumption of fruits and vegetables is not met by a significant portion of the population.

Including smoothies in your diet may be helpful if you are one of the many individuals who struggle to consume an adequate amount of fruits and vegetables daily. The fact that a single smoothie may include anywhere from two to three servings of fruit or vegetables makes it much simpler to achieve the goal.

➢ Increased Consumption of Fiber

In spite of the fact that the United States Department of Agriculture (USDA) recommended 25 to 38 grams of fiber per day, the typical American only consumes approximately 16 grams of fiber day. This is a significant problem since low fiber is associated with poor digestion and chronic diseases such as type II diabetes and heart disease.

Smoothies often include a high fiber concentration due to the high volume of fruit and vegetable ingredients. This may help bridge the gap between your typical fiber consumption and the amount recommended by the USDA, reducing your chance of developing chronic diseases and improving your overall health.

➢ Possible Dangers Involved with Smoothies

If you utilize a smoothie as a meal replacement most of the time, you won't need to worry about your health. The most significant issue that might arise while consuming smoothies is when they are substituted for other beverages accompanying meals. Because of this, consuming an excessive number of calories throughout the day is possible. Smoothies, on the other hand, have been shown to exacerbate the following conditions in some individuals:

➢ **Increased levels of glucose in the blood**

Sugars that are added to beverages that already contain a significant amount of sugar may be very harmful to your health and should be avoided wherever feasible. However, even if you make your smoothie at home using only natural ingredients, it can include a significant amount of sugar that occurs naturally. After all, the fruit has a naturally low high sugar content, and smoothies often include a significant amount of fruit.

Smoothies should be consumed with caution by those with type II diabetes or any other illness that makes sugar dangerous.

Making your juice

Basis for juicing

There is a large selection of nutrient-dense foods around the globe, including fruits, vegetables, herbs, and superfoods. In addition, juices may have a very diverse range of components, flavors, and nutritional profiles. It shouldn't be a secret how to create juice or make the best juice possible. Understanding the fundamentals is the most effective strategy for approaching the juicing activity.

And doing so is as simple as 1, 2, 3, and 4, as we will explain in more detail below. STEPS 1-4, to be specific.

NOTE: Make sure that the quantity of each ingredient you put into your juice corresponds to the number of the step in decreasing sequence. To put it another way, you should make use of the largest amount of the components described in step 1 and the smallest quantity of the components described in step 4.

First, choose your starting point.

The fruits and vegetables that are used to make up the "base" of the juice will provide the bulk of the juice that you drink. These are the components that result in the greatest amount of juice being produced.

The following are examples of "basic" substances that are used rather frequently:

➢ Cucumber (which has a very mellow and refreshing flavor)
➢ Celery (which has natural sodium and adds a fabulous salty flavor)
➢ Apple (for those of you who love your sweets)
➢ Pears, which also tend to be on the sweeter side and go particularly well with apples,
➢ Carrots (also on the sweeter side)
➢ If you have a longing for fruit juice, you may satisfy that urge with juice made from luscious fruits like melons, pineapples, or grapes. These fruits can either be the only component in the juice or act as the basis.

The second step is to include your leafy greens.

At Juice Guru, we strongly encourage our customers to consume green juice daily. And with the maximum amount of the "leafy green stuff" that can be packed into it. How much you use will be determined by your preference you are in the juicing process and the greens that you utilize.

To begin, there will be certain ground rules.

As is the case with everything else, we strongly suggest that you switch up the types of greens that you use each week to ensure that your juices have a sufficient amount of diversity (for the most varied nutrition). Additionally, you'll want to be selective about the kind of greens that you use... While some, if taken in excess, will ruin the flavor of your juice, others can be consumed in copious amounts without significantly altering the flavor.

It is essential to keep in mind that leafy greens may be included in ANY beverage, even the sugariest ones. If the flavor is the primary consideration for the juice that you are making, be sure to include the appropriate green ingredients.

Here are some guidelines.

Because of their subdued taste, the following types of greens may be used with complete abandon:

Spinach \Chard

Romaine lettuce, along with other types of lettuce

The following types of greens should be consumed in lower quantities due to their naturally bitter taste or other considerations:

> ➤ Dandelion greens (EXCELLENT nutrition, but VERY bitter)
> ➤ Collard greens (Also excellent but bitter)
> ➤ Kale (for those with thyroid issues, we recommend limiting or staying away from kale)

Step 3: Include more healthful fruits and vegetables in your diet.

Every single fruit and vegetable that can be juiced has its own set of advantages and may be included in to inr juicing routine. But some crops give less juice. Some might have an overwhelming impact, of some of them may be overpowering.

The following is a list of some of the most common extra fruits and vegetables that are juicy.

Broccoli is VERY high in dietary value, yet its flavor may be overbearing. One huge stalk should be used, and the green heads should be used for cooking and salads.

Beets are an excellent source of nutrition, but they have such a strong detoxifying effect that eating too much of them may make you feel ill. We suggest using no more than one-half of a beet for each big batch of cold-pressed juice.

Berries and grapes (You just cannot include enough of either of these in your juice. Juices made from blueberries and concord grapes, for instance, have been shown via extensive research to provide exceptional advantages to memory function. They also have a low glycemic index. However, they do not produce a significant amount of juice. Therefore, they are considered to be an add-on.)

The addition of red bell peppers to your rainbow juice will provide both a splash of color and a splash of nourishment. This vegetable is considered an add-on due to the spiciness of its taste.

In the fourth step, add any taste enhancers or boosters you like.

If you want a nice taste or an additional boost, use as many of the ingredients in this category as you desire, but keep in mind that you need to severely restrict the quantity you use since it is easy for them to overwhelm your juice.

Rule of thumb recommended by the Juice Guru about taste enhancers and boosts: Begin with a tiny quantity. You can ALWAYS add more. Once an excessive amount has been added, however, it is impossible to remove it.

Herbs that are fantastic for adding taste include cilantro, basil, and parsley, among others. If you use too much of it, the flavor of the parsley may become extremely overwhelming. However, parsley is an EXCELLENT source of nutrients.

➢ Ginger (just half an inch to an inch will do)
➢ Turmeric (same)
➢ Reishi, Ginseng, Maca, and other Adaptogens, Combined with Lemon and Lime (Brings Out Flavor in Any Juice Combination) Use roughly one per juice.)
➢ a hot pepper such as jalapeno or cayenne (Use sparingly to taste.)

Precautions for juices

When Making Juice in the Comfort of Your Own Home

➢ Before beginning and after finishing the preparation, you should use soap and warm water to wash your hands for at least twenty seconds.
➢ Remove any spots on fresh fruits and vegetables that are damaged or bruised with a knife. Toss out all of the vegetables that seem to be spoiling.
➢ Before chopping or cooking with any product, whether it was produced at home or purchased from a grocery shop or a farmer's market, be sure to thoroughly wash it under running water. It is not suggested to wash fruits and vegetables with soap, detergent, or any commercial produce wash before consumption.
➢ Scrub firm vegetables using a clean produce brush, such as watermelons and cucumbers. Even if you intend to peel the produce before using it for juicing, you should still wash it first to prevent any dirt or germs from sticking to the surface of the fruit from being transmitted into the juice.
➢ Following the washing step, drying the produce with a clean cloth towel or paper towel is an additional step that may help minimize the number of germs that may be present on the surface of the fruit.

Breakfast juice

1. POMEGRANATE, ORANGE, AND PINEAPPLE JUICE

Oranges and pomegranates are both loaded with vitamin C, potassium, and folate, three nutrients that give out a steady stream of energy over the day to keep you going strong.
Calories: 200 kcal/ 840 kj

Ingredients

- ½ Pomegranate
- 1 Orange
- 1/2 a Cup of Chopped Pineapple

Instructions

1. The pomegranate should be cut into four pieces, and the seeds should be removed and placed in a basin.
2. Remove the peel from the orange and cut the core out of the pineapple. Slice into suitable sizes.
3. In the juicer, place all of the ingredients.
4. Enjoy! If you'd like, pour it over some ice.

2. ORANGE LIGHT

This is the best juice for weight reduction because it contains both oranges, which are rich in vitamin C, and bok choy, which is rich in calcium.

Calories: 114 kcal/ 477 kj

Ingredients

- a third of a cup of bok choy
- 1/4 cup of sliced bananas
- ½ orange

Instructions

1. Oranges and bananas need to have their peels peeled off before they can be chopped.
2. After thorough washing, the bok choy leaves should be chopped into pieces that are about 2 inches long.
3. Insert items into the juicer.
4. Enjoy! If you'd like, pour it over some ice.

3. GREEN JUICE

The apple and orange in this dish are good sources of vitamin C, the cucumber and ginger help digestion, and the cherry tomatoes are delicious.
Calories: 150 kcal/ 630 kj

Ingredients

- Lots of Kale (you decide!)
- 1/2 Apple
- 1/2 Orange
- 1/2 Cucumber
- 1 piece of Ginger (about one inch)

Instructions

1. Remove the peel off the orange, then slice it into the necessary portions.
2. Apple and cucumber should both be sliced thinly.
3. Grate ginger to remove the skin.
4. Insert items into the juicer.
5. Enjoy! If you'd like, pour it over some ice.

4. LEMONADE AND BERRIES

Recipes for refreshing juices, such as berry lemon juice, may be found here.
White grapes, kiwi, strawberries, berries, and lemon are the five fruits that come together in this anti-fatigue drink recipe.
Calories: 323 kcal/ 1352 kj

Ingredients

- 1/3 of a cup's worth of white grapes
- 1/3 of a cup of kiwi
- 2 cups of whole strawberries
- ⅓ lemon
- 1/3 of berries

Instructions

1. Lemons and kiwis should both be peeled before being sliced into bite-sized pieces.
2. Wash everything carefully after removing the stems from the white grapes and the strawberry stems, respectively.
3. Wash and halve the berries
4. Juicers should have white grapes, kiwis, strawberries, berries, and lemons loaded into them.
5. Enjoy! If you'd like, pour it over some ice.

5. LEMON DETOX

Consume this lemon, banana, and pear juice to flush out dangerous toxins and aid in the body's natural healing process after strenuous exercise or a day of indulgence.
Calories: 287 kcal/ 1200 kj

Ingredients

- 1 and one-fourth cups of pear slices
- 1 sliced bananas
- ½ lemon

Instructions

1. Peel lemon and banana. Take out the pear seeds and remove the core. Cut into proper sizes.
2. Place one half of the pear, followed by the banana, then finish with the lemon in the juicer.
3. Put in the remaining portion of the pear.
4. Enjoy! If you'd like, pour it over some ice.

6. JUICE MADE FROM APPLES AND CUCUMBERS

This juice is loaded with beneficial ingredients for individuals who are battling digestive disorders, including cucumber, apple, lemon, and celery.
Calories: 131 kcal/ 548 kj

Ingredients

- 1/4 cup of sliced cucumbers
- half a cup of apples
- 1/4 of a cup of Lemon
- 1/4 cup of chopped celery
- (Optional) one to two fresh ginger pieces, each about two inches in length

Instructions

1. Remove the ends of the cucumber, then peel it and cut it into the necessary sizes using a knife.
2. After cutting the apple and removing its seeds, continue.
3. First, clean the celery by giving it a good wash.
4. Baking soda should be used to clean the lemon, and then it should be chopped up with the peel left on.
5. Peel ginger.
6. put the ingredients in the juicer.
7. *Insert the ingredients in the order they are listed above.
8. Enjoy! If you'd like, pour it over some ice.

7. KALE SPINACH JUICE

This dish has a little more sweetness to it, but it is ideal for serving children who might benefit from adding more greens to their diet.
Calories: 255 kcal/ 1070 kj

Ingredients

- a quarter of a pineapple
- A few little leaves of kale
- A fistful of chopped spinach
- (Optional - 1/2 lemon)
- 1 to 2 ginger pieces (each about 2 inches)

Instructions

1. Take the peel and core out of the pineapple, as well as trim and prepare the kale and spinach.
2. Pull the kale, spinach, and pineapple out in the sequence listed, then close the lever.
3. When you are ready to add the last ingredient, move the lever to the partially open position so that the compacted pulp may be released.
4. Enjoy! If you'd like, pour it over some ice.

8. JUICE MADE OF LEMON, CARROT, AND ORANGE

This energizing juice is perfect for combating stress and anxiety while simultaneously increasing levels of energy.
Calories: 340 kcal/ 1423 kj

Ingredients

- 2 Oranges
- 1/2 Lemon
- 4 Carrots
- 1 piece of Ginger

Instructions

1. Oranges and lemons should be peeled and sliced.
2. Ginger and carrots should both be peeled and chopped.
3. Put all of the ingredients into the juicer at once.
4. Enjoy! If you'd like, pour it over some ice.

9. GRAPEFRUIT, CARROT, GINGER

This juice, which was prepared in the kitchen of Martha Stewart, is an excellent way to perk up on a chilly morning, and it is an even more effective pick-me-up in the afternoon.
Calories: 380 kcal/ 1590 kj

Ingredients

- 2 grapefruits
- 5 miniature carrots
- 1 centimeter of fresh ginger

Instructions

1. Grapefruits and ginger should both be peeled and cut into acceptable sizes.
2. Peel the carrots and cut them into small pieces
3. The juicer should be loaded with all of the ingredients.
4. Enjoy! If you'd like, pour it over some ice.

10. DETOX WITH LEMON AND PEAR

It has a flavor that is light and creamy thanks to the banana and pear, and it has a hint of tartness from the lemon.
Calories: 215 kcal/ 900 kj

Ingredients

- 1 Pear
- 1/2 Lemon
- 1 Banana
- 1 piece Ginger approximately 1 inch (optional)

Instructions

1. Remove the peel from the pear, lemon, and ginger.
2. Peel and finely chop the ginger.
3. Bananas and lemons should be sliced.
4. Put everything that needs to be juiced into the juicer.
5. Enjoy! If you'd like, pour it over some ice.

11. Up Beet

This recipe produces a juice that is packed with vitamins and minerals, and it not only makes your taste buds happy but also strengthens your immune system.
Calories: 583 kcal/ 2440 kj

Ingredients

- 1 stalk of Celery
- 2 apples of a medium size
- 1 Beetroot
- 6 medium Carrots
- ½ cucumber
- ½ Lemon
- 1 big Orange
- Approximately 1.5 cups of whole Strawberries

Instructions

1. Lemon and orange must be peeled. Make the meat into slices.
2. Carrots, strawberries, beets, and cucumbers should all be chopped.
3. Use a juicer to process all of the ingredients.
4. After shaking or stirring the drink, serve.

Meal replacement smoothies

12. GREEN SMOOTHIE

Today is the perfect day to drink a green smoothie for the first time if you've never eaten one before. Because of the presence of leafy greens in them, smoothies made with these greens have a higher nutritional content than those made with other greens, making it possible to use a smoothie instead of any good meal.

Calories: 1244 kcal/ 5204 kj

Ingredients:

- 2 cups kale
- 2 cups of almond milk, sweetened to taste
- 2 cups of various berries
- 1 banana
- 2 tablespoons of butter made from almonds
- a quarter cup of rolled oats

Directions:

1. In a blender, combine the kale and the almond milk, and process until a creamy consistency is reached. Repeat the blending process with the remaining components.

13. BLUEBERRY, RASPBERRY AND BLACKBERRY SMOOTHIE

Enjoy eating berries? This is the perfect smoothie for someone like you. Not only is it an excellent meal replacement since it is filling, but it is also rich in antioxidants. It has a wonderful flavor as well!

Calories: 487 kcal/ 2037 kj

Ingredients:

- 1 ½ cups blueberries, frozen
- 1/3 cup of frozen raspberry chunks
- 1-third of a cup of frozen blackberries
- 1 and a half teaspoons worth of peanut butter
- 1 tablespoon and a half of honey
- 1 cup of milk

Instructions:

1. Place all of the ingredients in the blender and process them until the mixture reaches the required smoothness.

14. OVERNIGHT SMOOTHIE

When you're pressed for time in the morning but don't want to forgo breakfast, a smoothie like the one shown here is an excellent option. It's going to be perfect for you!

Calories:

Ingredients:

- Fruit from the freezer, your pick.
- 1 scoop protein powder
- 1 cup of milk
- 2 to 3 teaspoons of Greek yogurt in its basic form
- a quarter cup of uncooked oats and a quarter cup of raw spinach

instruction

1. Combine all of the ingredients, then put the mixture in the freezer to chill until the morning.

15. POTASSIUM PUNCH SMOOTHIE,

Because potassium helps to control blood pressure, it is essential for your body, and you should try to consume an adequate amount of the mineral. This smoothie is a great meal replacement, especially considering that skipping meals may lead to deficiencies.

Calories: 1039 kcal/ 4347 kj

Ingredients:

- 6 ounces of vanilla yogurt
- Water or milk
- ½ avocado
- 1 full peeled kiwi fruit
- 12 lime's worth of juice
- 1 to 2 cups of spinach, measured in heaping amounts
- between 1 and 2 tablespoons of honey
- cinnamon, one-fourth of a teaspoon

Directions:

Put everything in the blender except the liquid. Insert the right amount of liquid, water or milk to work the blender blades. Knead them until the mixture reaches the desired smoothness.

16. FRUIT AND SEEDS SMOOTHIE

What a satiating drink this smoothie is! This one is jam-packed with taste and essential nutrients, which will ensure that you are well-satiated after each meal.

Ingredients:

- 3 strawberries
- a tablespoon's worth of ground flaxseed
- 1 level spoonful of chia seed powder
- 1 scoop of raw protein
- 1 scoop ultra green formula
- 10 ounces of soy beverage
- Stevia, with or without

Directions:

1. Utilizing the blender, thoroughly combine all of the components until they become smooth. To be served chilled.

17. SMOOTHIES MADE WITH SUMMER STONE FRUITS

On a steamy summer day, this dish is just what you need to satisfy your hunger. It has a delicious flavor and provides a lot of fiber and other nutrients necessary to maintain your health and fitness.
Calories: 270 kcal/1130 kj

Ingredients:

- 1/2 cup of unflavored Greek yogurt
- 1 finely chopped prune
- 1 peach, cut into pieces
- ½ cup blueberries

Instructions

1. Put all of the ingredients in a blender and process until they form a homogeneous paste.

18. CARROT CAKE SMOOTHIE

Are you attempting to restrain yourself from ending the day with an unhealthy dessert? Here is something you may partake in to your heart's content without feeling the least bit guilty. It's incredibly delicious!

Calories: 394 kcal/ 1648 kj

Ingredients:

- ½ cup carrot juice
- 1 frozen banana
- ¾ cup unsweetened vanilla almond milk
- 1 scoop vanilla protein powder
- a quarter of a teaspoon of cinnamon
- 5 ice cubes

Directions:

1. In a blender, combine all of the ingredients and process until they form a smooth mixture.

19. ENERGY BOOSTING SMOOTHIE

Since Dr. Oz has provided you with this recipe, you can rest certain that it is both delicious and beneficial to your health. It is highly recommended that you give this smoothie a shot in the morning or at noon whenever you feel like you could use a little more pep in your step.

Calories: 445 kcal/ 1861 kj

Ingredients:

- 2 teaspoons cocoa powder
- 2 teaspoons of buttery peanut spread
- Greek yogurt measuring 8 ounces
- 1/2 cup ice
- 1 banana
- A little bit of cinnamon.

Directions:

1. Put the peanut butter, chocolate powder, yogurt, and ice into a blender and mix everything. After adding the banana, combine the mixture once more. Cinnamon should be sprinkled on top of the dish before serving.

20. CREAMY AVOCADO AND KALE SMOOTHIE

The avocado in this smoothie is a good source of potassium and fiber, all of which will assist you in feeling filled and prevent you from succumbing to hunger in the interim before your next meal. The addition of kale brings an abundance of beneficial nutrients and vitality. It has a wonderful flavor as well!

Calories: 674 kcal/ 2820 kj

Ingredients

- 1/2 avocado
- 1/2 cup kale
- 1 tablespoon cacao nibs
- half a cup of Greek yogurt
- 1/2 cup vanilla-flavored almond milk
- 1/2 cup frozen mango chunks
- 2 measuring tablespoons of honey

Directions:

1. Put all of the ingredients in a blender and process until they are completely combined and smooth.

21. STRAWBERRY, BANANA, AND OATMEAL SMOOTHIE

This meal-replacement smoothie for breakfast is without equal to any other meal-replacement smoothie that has ever been created. Oatmeal offers a pleasing texture and a lot of satisfying fiber, which complements the delicious combination of bananas and strawberries.

Calories: 430 kcal/ 1800 kj

Ingredients:

- 1/2 cup of almond milk that has not been sweetened
- 1/2 cup pomegranate juice
- 1 scoop protein powder
- 1 cup of baby spinach that has been freshly packed.
- 1/2 banana
- a single cup's worth of frozen strawberries
- 1/4 cup of rolled oats made in the traditional way

Directions:

1. Using a blender, make a smooth purée of the almond milk, pomegranate juice, protein powder, and spinach. After adding the banana, strawberries, and oats, combine the mixture once more.

22. SMOOTHIE MADE WITH ALMONDS, BANANAS, AND FLAX SEEDS

The plant-based proteins in almonds are among the most beneficial and beneficial that Mother Nature has to offer. They have a high vitamin and mineral content, are proven to reduce cholesterol levels, and are filled with antioxidants.

Bananas are well-known for several health benefits, including their high fiber, natural sweetness, and high levels of antioxidants. They boost the flavor as well as the creaminess and flavor of the smoothie that you make with them.

Flax seeds are rich in omega-3 fats, which have been shown to lessen the chance of acquiring some malignancies as well as reduce blood pressure.

If you are a fan of almonds and bananas, this is one of the smoothies you must include in your morning or lunch routine.

Calories: 519 kcal/ 2171 kj

Ingredients:

- 2 big bananas, either thawed or fresh from the freezer
- 1 teaspoon and a half of almond butter
- 2 tablespoons of ground flax seeds
- ½ cup almond milk
- 1 milliliter of honey or pure maple syrup

Directions:

1. Blend all of the ingredients until they are completely combined, then serve the mixture cold.

23. SMOOTHIE MADE WITH SPINACH, MANGO, AND CARROTS TO DRINK

Working out is a wonderful activity since it is such an effective means of weight reduction. In addition to this, you trigger the production of endorphins, which work to alleviate stress and foster a general feeling of well-being.

It is now time to give your body something scrumptious and nourishing to help it refresh.

You need to educate yourself on how to make meal replacement shakes at home if you want to maintain your current weight and state of health. You don't need much more than a decent blender and a few basic ingredients to whip up a delicious smoothie.

The smoothie made with spinach, mango, and carrots is loaded with vitamin, nutritional, and antioxidant-rich ingredients. During exercise, your body will replace any fluids that are lost, and it will also enhance the functioning of your digestive system.

Calories: 599 kcal/ 2506 kj

Ingredients:

- 2 cups of fresh baby spinach
- 1 cup frozen mangoes
- 1/2 cup of chopped baby carrots
- 1/2 cup of plain yogurt that is low in fat
- ¼ cup orange juice
- ½ cup coconut water
- 2 oranges (peeled)

Directions:

1. Put all of the ingredients in a blender, and blend them until the mixture is silky smooth. Serve.

24. SMOOTHIE MADE WITH OATMEAL, BANANAS, AND STRAWBERRIES

Oatmeal is the one food item that you absolutely must always have on hand in your home. Why? Oats, in their whole form, are beneficial to the success of any weight reduction program. They contain a lot of soluble fiber and are healthy all around.

Strawberries are not only delicious but also have a high vitamin content and may be used to cure gout and arthritis.

This is one of those nutritious smoothies for supper that enables you to sleep better since you won't be hungry when you get up in the morning. This is because both oats and bananas are satisfying, making them an ideal replacement for a hearty meal.

Calories: 1200 kcal/ 5020 kj

Ingredients:

- 1/2 cup of unprocessed oats
- 1 cup almond milk
- 1/2 a cup of non-flavored low-fat yogurt
- 2 measuring cups' worth of frozen strawberries
- 2 ripe bananas
- 1 teaspoon of honey
- 1/2 tsp vanilla extract

Directions:

1. Put all of the ingredients into a blender and process until everything is well combined, then serve.

25. SMOOTHIE MADE WITH PEANUT BUTTER, BANANAS, AND JELLY.

Did you know that eating peanut butter regularly may help keep your heart healthy?
Second, it is beneficial to the process of bodybuilding! If you want to put on more muscle, you should make this one of your go-to smoothie recipes to use instead of meals daily.
Calories: 424 kcal/ 1774 kj

Ingredients:

- 1 ripe banana
- ½ cup almond milk
- two tablespoons of peanut butter
- 1 cup of a frozen mixture of berries

Directions:

Combine all of the ingredients in a blender until they are silky smooth. Serve.

26. SMOOTHIE WITH AVOCADO AND BANANA, HIGH IN PROTEIN

Avocado lover? Then you've got yourself a recipe for what may very well be the finest lunch smoothie of all time!

There's a reason why avocados are such a popular cuisine ingredient: they're delicious. They are rich in heart-healthy fatty acids, potassium, and fiber, all of which are abundant in these nuts. Avocados, much like oats, have a reputation for being quite filling.

Calories: 419 kcal/ 1753 kj

Ingredients:

- 1 cup almond milk
- 1/3 ripe and frozen avocado
- ½ ripe banana
- 1/4 cup of powdered whey protein
- 1 tsp flax

Directions:

Put all of the ingredients in a blender and process until they are smooth and evenly combined. Serve.

27. BLUEBERRY AND COCONUT MILK SMOOTHIE MADE WITH BLUEBERRIES

If you want to lose weight, you should increase the amount of coconut milk that you drink. Coconut milk contains auric acid, which helps to strengthen the immune system and inhibits the formation of cancer cells.

If you add some blueberries, which are naturally low in calories, you will have the ideal ingredient for a smoothie.

Calories: 354 kcal/ 1481 kj

Ingredients:

- 1/2 cup of whole, fresh blueberries
- ½ cup plain coconut milk
- 1 teaspoon of honey
- 1 tsp lemon juice

Directions:

Put all of the ingredients in a blender and mix them. After thoroughly combining, serve.

28. PROTEIN SMOOTHIE MADE WITH SPINACH, BANANAS, AND FLAX

There are so many different recipes for meal-replacement shakes that it is almost hard to find one that does not include spinach as an ingredient.

The reason for this is that spinach is loaded with iron. Iron is necessary for the development of oxygen-rich red blood cells, which iron helps to sustain. Spinach is an essential component in managing diabetes and is responsible for supplying the body with essential nutrients such as magnesium and calcium.

Therefore, wash your spinach and enjoy this nutritious smoothie that is rich in protein.

Calories: 386 kcal/ 1615 kj

Ingredients:

- 1 cup spinach
- 2 ripe bananas
- 1 tablespoon of organic pea protein powder from NutriBullet
- 1 tbs flax seeds
- ½ cup almond milk

Directions:

Use a blender to combine all of the ingredients. To be served cold.

29. PUMPKIN PROTEIN SMOOTHIE WITH PUMPKIN AND GINGER

Pumpkin is another superfood that assists in the process of shedding excess weight. In addition to that, it has a high vitamin A content and a high antioxidant content.

Ginger is a common item found in kitchen cupboards, and it is used to cure various ailments, including nausea, muscular discomfort, and inflammation.

This is one of the most convenient recipes for making smoothies to use as a meal replacement since all components can be found easily.

Calories: 118 kcal/ 491 kj

Ingredients:

- 1 cup pumpkin purée
- 1 ripe frozen banana
- 1/4 of a teaspoon of ground ginger root
- 1/4 teaspoon of cinnamon powder
- ¼ tsp vanilla powder

Directions:

Put all of the ingredients in a blender and give it a good mix. The necessary consistency may then be achieved by adding some water, after which it can be served.

30. SMOOTHIE MADE WITH AVOCADO, SPINACH, AND KIWI

This smoothie is not only an excellent alternative for meal replacement, but it also cleanses your body from the inside out.

Because it is rich in fiber and vitamins, kiwi enhances the positive effects that avocado and spinach have on one's health. It is rich in vitamin C, which protects against damage to the body that might lead to cancer.

You might use this as one of your healthy smoothies for supper because it is satiating and has detoxifying characteristics. Best taken an hour before bed.

Calories: 618 kcal/ 2586 kj

Ingredients:

- 1 cup spinach
- 3 kiwis, peeled and sliced, for garnish
- 1/2 of a ripe avocado, either fresh or frozen
- ½ cup almond or coconut milk
- 3 tablespoons of natural honey
- 1 cup of ice

Directions:

Mix all of the ingredients in a blender until they become creamy. Enjoy!

31. CHOCOLATE BERRY SMOOTHIE WITH CHOCOLATE AND BERRIES

This chocolate-flavored healthy smoothie is going to blow your mind if you have a serious obsession with chocolate.

Chocolates, in addition to being scrumptious, also provide a plethora of different advantages for one's health. They are loaded with antioxidants, lower the chance of developing cardiovascular disease, and shield the skin from the damaging effects of the sun.

The same is true for berries, which are well-recognized for their ability to bring cholesterol levels down.

This is one of the greatest lunch smoothies, and drinking it as you work will help you resist the need to snack on bad foods.

Calories: 765 kcal/ 3200 kj

Ingredients:

- 2 milligrams of cocoa powder
- a quarter cup's worth of frozen berries
- 1 ripe banana
- 1 tablespoon of chia seeds
- 1 cup of coconut milk, almond milk, or soy milk
- 1 tablespoon of maple syrup or honey
- 1 cup of ice

Directions:

Put all of the ingredients in a blender and process until they are completely smooth. Immediately serve after cooking.

Detoxifying and cleansing juice

32. THE MORNING ENERGIZER JUICE

This revitalizing concoction of apple, lemon, ginger, and cayenne pepper is a great way to get you to cleanse off to a good start in the morning.
Calories: 88 kcal/ 368 kj

Ingredients

- 12 ounces lemon
- 0.18 oz ginger
- 1 little sprinkle of ground cayenne pepper

Directions

1.79   Step one: wash the fruit and vegetables.
2. Weigh ingredients.
3. Remove the rind of the lemon. If you keep the peel on, the taste will be more bitter.
4. Combine all of the ingredients and juice them.
5. Sprinkle a generous amount of cayenne pepper over the mixture.

Pro Tips

It's up to you whether or not you want to peel the lemon. We find it easiest to "skip peel" them, which is simply coarsely chopping off the peel while leaving part of it to remain. This reduces the amount of time needed for preparation, and the little amount of peel adds flavor!

33. JUICE MADE FROM CARROTS, APPLES, AND GINGER

This recipe for carrot juice is not only simple to prepare, but it also provides several benefits to one's health. The combination of carrot, lemon, apple, and ginger in this recipe is sure to please your taste buds.

Calories: 249 kcal/ 1041 kj

Ingredients

- 13.2 ounces of carrot
- Apple, red, 3.85 ounces
- 2 ounces green apple
- 0.35-ounce lemon
- 0.35 ounces of ginger

Directions

1. Step one: weigh the ingredients after they have been washed.
2. Cut the tops off of the carrots and set them aside.
3. Remove the rinds of the lemons.
4. Put the items in your juicer and press the juice out.

Pro Tips

Because it might be difficult to get all of the dirt off of the tops of the carrots, it is a good idea in my book to cut them off.

If you want the lemon to have a more subtle taste, peel it. If you want juices with a more robust taste or more body, you should ground them with the peel on.

34. HEALTHIEST AND MOST DELICIOUS GREEN JUICE

This delicious green juice recipe, which was developed by Chef Ari Sexner, is not only nutritious and low in calories, but it also tastes fantastic!
Calories: 95 kcal/ 397 kj

Ingredients

- 5 oz kale
- 5 ounces cucumber
- 1-ounce green apple
- 1 ounces celery
- 0.92-ounce lemon
- 0.48 oz ginger

Directions

1.84   Step one: weigh the vegetables after it has been washed.
2. Remove the rind of the lemon.
3. Pulverize all of the ingredients and force them through your juicer.

Pro Tips

When at all feasible, go for organically grown foods. Not only is it better for you from a nutritional standpoint, but it also tastes better.

Be careful to extract the juice from the cucumber while leaving the peel on (remove the peel if the cucumber is not organic) since the peel contains beta-carotene, which is an essential antioxidant that the body may convert into vitamin A.

35. THE TRADITIONAL BEET JUICE

This time-honored dish is a favorite among many athletes since beet juice offers a plethora of wonderful benefits, including the enhancement of stamina and blood flow as well as an increase in energy levels.

Calories: 88 kcal/ 368 kj

Ingredients

- 7 ounces of red beet
  - 3 ounces orange
  - 1 oz kale
  - 1-ounce cucumber

Direction

1. Step one: weigh the vegetables after it has been washed.
2. Remove the rind from the oranges and trim the stem ends of the beets.
3. Combine all of the ingredients and juice them together.

Pro Tip

Take off the top ends, then thoroughly wipe both sides of the bottoms. When they are on the smaller side, I cut off the slender bottom section as well.

36. GOLDEN SWEET GREEN JUICE

This recipe for sweet green juice is simple to produce and serves as an excellent introduction to green juice for those who are just starting. Also a fan favorite among children!
Calories: 192 kcal/ 803 kj

Ingredients

- 9.75 ounces of pineapple is required
- 5.73 ounces cucumber
- ounces of green apple
- 24 milligrams of fresh mint leaves

Direction

1. Step one: weigh the vegetables after it has been washed.
2. Chop the pineapple into bite-sized pieces. Leave the peel on the pineapple if you're going to be using a Good nature juice press.
3. Combine all of the ingredients and juice them together.

Pro Tips

If you are using a Good nature juice press, you should keep the pineapple peel on. It has a very high concentration of nutrients that are of great benefit to the body.

When loading the product into the grinder hopper, it is preferable to use a combination of greens and softer fruits like pineapple. This ensures that the food is ground to the appropriate consistency. This results in a finer grinding of the greens, ultimately yielding more juice. Keep two or three apple chunks aside for the very end of the process since apples are excellent for cleaning the grinder and pushing through any remaining pieces of mint or pineapple that may have been stuck in the process.

37. HOMEMADE V8 JUICE

You may make your homemade version of V8 juice that is low in salt and nutritious for you. It should be loaded with vitamins, minerals, and enzymes.
Calories: 50 kcal/ 209 kj

Ingredients Tomatoes, 11.46 ounces total

- ounces carrot
- ounces celery
- 0.71-ounce romaine
- 0.63 ounces of spinach
- 0.36-ounce parsley
- 14 ounces of watercress
- 0.11-ounce red beet
- 0.08-ounce garlic
- 0.63 ounces spinal direction
1. Step one: weigh the vegetables after it has been washed.
2. Cut off the tops of the carrots and beets and set them aside.
3. Combine all of the ingredients and juice them together.

Pro Tips

When used as a foundation for a cold-pressed Bloody Mary drink, this juice has a delicious flavor. Looking for something with a little bit more of a salty flavor? You may want to add additional celery. You should eat the stems along with the leafy greens since they often contain a great deal of taste and juice. When they are fresh from the farm, leafy greens often have the most dirt on their leaves. Therefore, it is important to wash them properly.

Be sure to cut off the tops of the beets and thoroughly clean the bottoms. If they are on the small side, you should also cut off the slender bottom half.

38. TRADITIONAL ALMOND MILK

This is a classic that has stood the test of time. On a juice cleanse, the nicest thing to have for dessert is homemade almond milk that has been cold-pressed.
Calories: 112,8 kcal/ 472 kj

Ingredients

- 10.65 ounces of water with ice
- 0.30 ounces raw almonds
- 0.70 oz pitted dates
1. 0.08 ounces vanilla extract

2. Instructions

3. The day before you want to make this dish, put the almonds in a container, fill it with water until it covers them, and let them soak in the refrigerator for a full day. Add the dates to the water during the last hour of the soaking process to rehydrate.
4. Pour out the water in the bowl containing the almonds and dates, then rinse and drain them once more.
5. Combine all of the ingredients and juice them together.
6. Combine the almonds, dates, and 10.65 ounces of water in a blender.
7. Pour the slurry into the press bag, making sure it is no more than a third full, and then press the mixture.

Pro Tips

For the vanilla, you can use vanilla pods, and grind them in a blender along with almonds and water. Experiment with it and make it your own by adding various extracts or herbs, such as lavender.

39. GREEN BEET CLEANSE

This beverage, which is abundant in vitamins A, K, C, and E, is what your liver thinks about as it goes to sleep at night. Oh, but wait... unless you flush out your liver with this juice, it will never have a chance to relax.
Calories: 119 kcal/ 498 kj

Ingredients

- 1 carrot,
- 1 yellow beet,
- 2 celery stalks,
- 1 medium cucumber

Direction

Run all of the ingredients through a juicer, and then swirl the mixture very well to incorporate everything.

40. VEGGIE VITAE

When you are producing this delicious juice, it is best to process the cucumber towards the very end of the procedure. Because it has a high percentage of water, it will assist in flushing the juices extracted from the leaves through the pulp and into your glass.
Calories: 293 kcal/ 1228 kj

Ingredients

- One-half pound of spinach
- Two celery stalks with leaves
- Three carrots with their tops attached
- One half of an apple
- One miniature cucumber

Direction

The juicer should be used to process all of the ingredients, but you should save the cucumber for last. To blend, give it a good stir.

Beet Juice Supreme

This earthy juice benefits from the addition of celery's pleasant brightness.
Calories: 132 kcal/ 552 kj

Ingredients

- Two beets,
- one tomato,
- two celery stalks,
- one cucumber is included.

Direction

Run all of the ingredients through a juicer and then swirl the mixture very well to incorporate everything.

41. DANDELION DELIGHT

In this juice with a vibrant taste, saving the delicious flesh of the cucumber for last ensures that more of the juice and nutrients from the leafy greens are extracted.
Calories: 372 kcal/ 1556 kj

Ingredients

- Two stalks of celery,
- two cups of spinach,
- one cup of dandelion greens,
- three leaves of kale,
- one cup of parsley,
- one cucumber

direction

The juicer should be used to process all of the ingredients, but you should save the cucumber for last. To blend, give it a good stir.

42. FENNEL AND GREENS

This juice has a great peppery and licorice taste thanks to the addition of fennel, which is often featured in many Italian cuisines.
Calories: 372 kcal/ 1556 kj

Ingredients

- 3 carrots
- 1/2 pound each of spinach and kale leaves
- 1 clove of garlic
- 1/2 bulb of fennel, the leaves and stem
- 1/2 lemon
- 1/2 teaspoon of cayenne pepper

Direction

A juicer should be used to process the carrots, spinach, kale, and garlic first, followed by the fennel, and finally the lemon. After adding the cayenne to the juice, give it a good toss to blend the two ingredients.

43. BRING SOME LIFE TO YOUR LIVER JUICE

Even the pleasant appearance of this one will put a smile on your liver's face. You won't be able to get enough of this juice since not only is it high in nutritious content, but it also has a tonne of delicious taste. When you process the apple last, you'll help force extra liquid and nutrients from the root veggies through into your juice. This is because the apple will be processed last.
Calories: 235 kcal/ 983 kj

Ingredients

- Two beets
- Two carrots
- One apple
- One-quarter of a teaspoon of ground cinnamon
- One-inch piece of ginger

Direction

Using a juicer, first process the beets, carrots, and ginger, and then add the apple. After adding the cinnamon to the juice, give it a good toss to blend the two ingredients.

44. COCKTAIL FOR DETOXIFICATION

In many cultures, cabbage is consumed to clean up the digestive system. If you like a little heat, a jalapeno pepper can turn a jalapeno rink into a party in a glass.
Calories: 284 kcal/ 1188 kj

Ingredients

- 1 broccoli head
- 2 green bell peppers
- 1/2 head green cabbage
- 2 tomatoes

Direction

In a juicer, begin by juicing the broccoli, then go on to the green bell peppers and cabbage, and finish with the tomatoes. To blend, give it a good stir.

45. ANTIOXIDANTS PLUS

The flavor of this beverage brings to mind a substantial vegetable stew. When you process the tomatoes last, you'll help force more liquid and nutrients from the other components through into your juice. This will ensure that you get the most out of your tomato juice.

Calories: 402 kcal/ 1682 kj

Ingredients

- 6 leaves of kale
- 2 cups of spinach
- 1 celery stalk
- 2 green bell peppers
- 3 carrots
- 1/4 an onion
- 1/2 of a beet
- 1/2 of a garlic bulb
- 2 tomatoes

Instruction

Use a juicer to process all of the ingredients but save the tomatoes for processing last. To blend, give it a good stir.

46. ORANGE PINEAPPLE CHILI

This fruit juice has just the right amount of sweetness for breakfast. Not only is it beneficial for your gut, but it may also be used as an effective remedy for getting rid of a cold.
Calories: 291 kcal/ 1217 kj

Ingredients

- Two carrots,
- one orange,
- one-fourth of a pineapple,
- one-half of a teaspoon of cayenne pepper

instruction

First, the carrots go through the juicer, followed by the orange and the pineapple. After adding the cayenne to the juice, give it a good toss to blend the two ingredients.

47. DELICIOUS CARROTS WITH SPINACH.

Even though the hue of this juice isn't very appealing to the eye, you will be pleasantly pleased by how sweet it tastes. However, it does an excellent job of cleansing out your colon!
Calories: 242 kcal/ 1012 kj

Ingredients

- Two cups of spinach
- One-half of a sweet potato
- Three carrots

Instruction

First, the spinach is put through the juicer, followed by the sweet potato and the carrots. To blend, give it a good stir.

48. JUICE PREPARED FROM BROCCOLI CHOKE

This juice combination will not only delight your taste but also do wonders for your colon. It is fantastic for providing increased vitamins and a little bit of vegetable protein. In this process step, adding a little water to the processing of the broccoli and artichoke helps extract the maximum amount of nutrients from those vegetables.

Calories: 213 kcal/ 891 kj

Ingredients

- One chopped broccoli head
- One chopped artichoke
- One chopped carrot
- One minced garlic clove
- One cup of water

Instruction

Follow the processing of the broccoli in the juicer with a quarter cup of water. After the artichoke has been processed, add another quarter cup of water. After that, put the carrot and garlic through the food processor, and add the remaining half cup of water. To blend, give it a good stir.

49. LEAFY GREEN DELIGHT

This juice is loaded with a variety of beneficial vitamins and minerals thanks to the greens that it contains. This is the best possible combination for detoxifying and cleaning out the intestines. Calories: 186 kcal/ 778 kj

Ingredients

- Six leaves of kale,
- one cup of spinach,
- one cup of collard greens
- 1 small red bell pepper
- 1 clove of garlic

Direction

Run all of the ingredients through a juicer, and then swirl the mixture very well to incorporate everything.

50. COCKTAIL MADE WITH CUCUMBERS AND CARROTS

Because lemon juice helps prevent oxidation, this is a wonderful juice to take with you while you are on the road for lunch, as it will keep the juice fresh for longer.

Calories: 292 kcal/ 1222 kj

Ingredients

- 1 cucumber
- 4 carrots
- 1 apple
- 1 lemon

Direction

Utilize a juicer to process all of the components. As soon as possible, swirl the mixture completely but gently to properly distribute the lemon juice without introducing any oxygen-containing air.

51. GREEN BEAST

The mix of ingredients in this juice creates a unique nutritional profile that is hard to obtain in other beverages, and it also has a wonderful flavor. If you want to give it a little more kick, mix half a teaspoon of cayenne pepper or black pepper into the juice.
Calories: 236 kcal/ 987 kj

Ingredients

- three leaves of kale
- one cup of spinach
- six heads of Brussels sprouts
- three stalks of celery
- one carrot
- one cucumber

Direction

A juicer should first be used to process the kale, spinach, and Brussels sprouts, followed by the celery, carrot, and cucumber. To blend, give it a good stir.

52. SPROUTS OF PEPPER

This juice has a taste that is lively and crisp, and it has a great cooling effect. Because it provides a decent nutritious boost without making you feel heavy, it is an excellent option for lunch. It is possible to extract the entire taste of the basil into the juice by processing the celery and peppers after the herb has been used.

Calories: 196 kcal/ 829 kj

Ingredients

- One cup of alfalfa sprouts
- Six sprouts of the Brussels kind
- Two sprigs of basil
- Four stalks of celery
- Two green bell peppers

Direction

Using a juicer, begin by processing the alfalfa sprouts, Brussels sprouts, and basil leaves. Next, add the celery and bell peppers. To blend, give it a good stir.

53. CLEANSE WITH CRANBERRIES AND WATERMELON

Because of their antibacterial properties, cranberries are an excellent addition to this dish. As a result, they help flush out your kidneys and protect them from infection.
Calories: 280 kcal/ 1171 kj

Ingredients

- Two sprigs of mint
- One cup's worth of cranberries
- Two cups' worth of watermelon

Direction

First, the mint is put through the juicer, followed by the cranberries, and finally the watermelon. To blend, give it a good stir.

54. TEA MADE WITH WATERMELON SEEDS

Even though it isn't strictly a juice, this is one of the most effective treatments that modern medicine has discovered to help prevent kidney stones, clean your kidneys and urinary system, and stimulate kidneys that aren't working properly. If you have a history of kidney stones, you need to consume at least three cups of this tea every single week.

Ingredients

- One tablespoon of watermelon seeds that have been crushed
- Eight ounces of water brought to a boil

Direction

After pouring the boiling water over the watermelon seeds, let the seeds soak in the water for as long as it takes for the water to return to room temperature. Then you may eat it.

55. LEMONADE

This is utilized by leading treatment and research centers for kidney stones to both control and prevent the formation of kidney stones. If you feel the need to, you may sweeten it up a little bit by adding some honey to it.
Calories: 116 kcal/ 485 kj

Ingredients

- One cup of water
- Four lemons

Direction

First, the lemons are put through a juicer, and then water is added. To blend, give it a good stir.

56. JUICE OF ENVY

This juice is exceptionally mouthwatering in its deliciousness. It has a wonderful kick, and the cucumber lends it a crisp, clean taste rounded out by the apple and mint for a touch of sweetness.
Calories: 259 kcal/ 1083 kj

Ingredients

- A piece of ginger measuring one inch;
- A sprig of mint;
- Two green apples;
- One cucumber

Direction

First, the ginger and the mint are put through a juicer, followed by the apples and the cucumber. To blend, give it a good stir.

57. CRAN BEET WATERMELON

This detoxifying juice will offer you a nice energy boost without the crash that often follows, making it an excellent choice for either lunch or a snack in the afternoon.
Calories: 212 kcal/ 887 kj

Ingredients

- One beet
- One cup of sliced watermelon
- One cup of cranberries

Instruction

First, the beet is put through the juicer, followed by the cranberries, and finally the watermelon. To blend, give it a good stir.

58. LEMONADE WITH CRANBERRIES

It is very nice to drink this juice when it is warm out since it is not heavy and is refreshing. Your digestive system will thank the cranberries for their antioxidant and anti-inflammatory characteristics. Cranberries will make your digestive tract extremely happy.
Calories: 167 kcal/ 699 kj

Ingredients

- One cup of fresh or frozen cranberries
- Two lemons
- Two glasses of water

Direction

Cranberries and lemons are first put through a juicer, after which water is added. To blend, give it a good stir.

59. SMOOTHIE MADE WITH STRAWBERRY AND BANANA.

Because bananas include fiber, you can't drink this during a juice fast, but if you're simply searching for something incredibly beneficial for your kidneys, you can't go wrong with this smoothie! Because of the additional advantages that the fibrous pulp may bring, this one is treated in a blender.

Calories: 233 kcal/ 975 kj

Ingredients

- 6 strawberries
- 1 banana
- 1 pomegranate

Instruction

Put the banana and strawberries in a blender and mix until smooth. After you have seeded the pomegranate and collected its juice, put the pulp and juice in the blender. To make a smoothie out of the mixture, run it through the blender and, if necessary, add more water to thin it down.

60. SPROUT OF CELERY AND PEPPER

This juice benefits your kidneys and immune system, particularly the immunological system. The taste is refreshing and not overpowering.
Calories: 256 kcal/ 1071 kj

Ingredients

- Three cups' worth of alfalfa sprouts
- Four green bell peppers
- Four stalks' worth of celery
- One cucumber

Instruction

In a juicer, first process the alfalfa sprouts, then add the bell peppers, celery, and cucumber. Process until smooth. To blend the ingredients without introducing air that may cause oxidation, stir them carefully but completely.

61. A BLAST OF BERRY AND MELON.

This delicious juice is made more refreshing by the addition of cucumber, which also helps to reduce the sweetness of the drink.
Calories: 328 kcal/ 1372 kj

Ingredients

- Six strawberries
- One cup of sliced honeydew melons
- One cup of blueberries
- One cucumber

Instruction

Run all of the ingredients through a juicer, and then swirl the mixture very well to incorporate everything.

62. LEMONADE WITH CHERRY AND BERRY BLEND

Because the oxidation process is slowed down by the lemon juice, you won't have to worry about the juice's nutritional content degrading as quickly if you take it with you on the go for lunch. Adding the lemon at the end of the juicing process, it will assist in forcing extra liquid and nutrients from the other components through into the juice.
Calories: 382 kcal/ 1598 kj

Ingredients

- 1 cup sour cherries
- 1 cup raspberries
- 1 cup blueberries
- 1 lemon

Instruction

Use a juicer to process all of the ingredients, but hold off on adding the lemon until last. To blend, give it a good stir.

63. CHILLED PLUM AND MELON DRINK

A refreshing glass of this juice is just the thing to cool you down on a hot summer day. If you will serve it to other people, garnish it with a sprig of mint.
Calories: 205 kcal/ 858 kj

Ingredients

- 2 plums
- 1 cup cubed watermelon
- 1 cucumber

direction

Run all of the ingredients through a juicer, and then swirl the mixture very well to incorporate everything.

64. GUAVALOUPE GOODIE

This wonderful glass of juice packed with nutrients is just as simple to prepare as it is to consume.
Calories: 411 kcal/ 1720 kj

Ingredients

- 6 carrots
- 1 guava
- 1 cup diced cantaloupe

Instruction

First, the carrots are put through the juicer, followed by the guava and the cantaloupe. To blend, give it a good stir.

65. GREEN SHIELD

When preparing the asparagus for juicing, use the same steps as when preparing it for cooking: hold each spear at each end and gently bend it until the stalk breaks naturally; then, remove the tough ends. If you like things on the spicy side, put jalapeno in the juicer or a half teaspoon of cayenne pepper in your glass. Both of these will give this juice a nice kick.
Calories: 245 kcal/ 1025 kj

Ingredients

- one bunch of asparagus, with the ends, removed
- four green bell peppers
- six stalks of celery
- one lemon

Direction

First, the asparagus is put through the juicer, followed by the green bell peppers, celery, and finally the lemon. To blend, give it a good stir.

Vegetable juice

66. CARROT, CUCUMBER, CELERY, AND APPLE JUICE

Calories: 219 kcal/ 916 kj

Ingredients

- 3 carrots
- 1 apple
- 1 celery stick
- ¼ a cucumber
- ½ a lemon

Procedure:

1. It is essential to thoroughly wash all of the components to eliminate any traces of pesticides or fertilizers that may have been used in the production of the veggies.
2. To begin, trim the ends of the carrots and celery, and then remove the core from the apple. They need to be cut into tiny pieces, well mixed, and then placed in a juicer or blender.

67. JUICE MADE FROM CARROTS, TOMATOES, AND APPLE

Calories: 409 kcal/ 1711 kj

Ingredients:

- 6 carrots
- 2 apples
- 2 plum tomatoes
- A little bit of ginger

Procedure:
Use a juicer to combine the carrots and apples, and then sprinkle on some ground ginger before serving. First, ensure that the carrots and apples have been well washed and removed any unnecessary portions.

68. JUICE MADE WITH BROCCOLI, CARROTS, APPLES, AND BEETROOTS

Calories: 210 kcal/ 879 kj

Ingredients:

- Broccoli 225g
- Carrots 170g
- Beetroot 55g
- Apples 55g
- Honey may be added for a sweeter flavor, although this step is optional.

Procedure:

Be careful to wash the broccoli, carrots, beets, and apples before eating them. To get rid of any pesticides on them, it is preferable to soak them in water for at least half an hour before preparing them.

After that, trim the tough ends off the carrots and break the broccoli into florets with a floret separator. After slicing the beets and using the juicer to extract their juice, combine the other ingredients and serve.

69. REFRESHING BLEND OF GREEN JUICE

Calories: 216 kcal/ 904 kj

Ingredients:

- 9 ounces of unripe green apples
- Exactly 4.5 ounces of broccoli
- Three ounces of celery
- 1 ounce of chopped parsley
- Cucumber measuring 6 ounces

Procedure:

To remove any possible traces of pesticides, thoroughly wash each component. They should be cut into little pieces, and any tricky bits should be removed. Make use of a juicer, in addition to a big glass.

Apples were washed, cored, and then sliced into bite-sized pieces. Make florets out of the broccoli by separating them. Remove the ends from the celery and set them aside. Complete the drink by juicing the ingredients and serving it over ice.

70. A MIXTURE OF FRESH SPINACH, APPLE, AND LEMON JUICE

Calories : 270 kcal/ 1129kj

Ingredients:

- 1 bunch of spinach
- 2 apples
- 1/2 lemon, peeled (optional)

Procedure:

Place all of the ingredients inside the juicer. Extracting juice from greens is best done using a juicer that has two sets of gears. Combine everything carefully, then savor it.

Antiaging juice

71. ORANGE CARROT

This vivid orange drink, which is both simple and effective, can improve your eyesight (as well as your appearance) for many years to come.
Calories: 309 kcal/ 1293 kj

Ingredients

- One yellow beet in total
- 6 carrots
- 1 orange

Instruction

In a juicer, first process the beets and carrots, and then add the orange. Combine everything by giving it a thorough stir.

72. THE DRINK OF BUGS

To recreate this scene, you need to do what Bugs Bunny did and kick back some carrots. The use of watercress in this preparation results in a juice that has a distinctive spicy taste.
Calories: 406 kcal/ 1699 kj

Ingredients

- One bouquet of watercress in total
- 1 cup spinach
- One whole broccoli head
- 1 squash
- 5 carrots

Instruction

The watercress, spinach, and broccoli are first put through the juicer, followed by the squash and the carrots. Combine everything by giving it a thorough stir.

73. JUICE TO THE C TO SEE

Note that certain rigorous juice diets won't accept cantaloupe because of the quantity of pulp that slips through, yet cantaloupe is incredibly excellent for you despite this.
Calories: 350 kcal/ 1466 kj

Ingredients

- 2 sweet potatoes
- 2 carrots
- 1 squash
- 1 cup cantaloupe

Instruction

First, the squash and cantaloupe are put through the juicer, followed by the sweet potatoes and carrots. Combine everything by giving it a thorough stir.

74. THE PLEASURE IS ALL MINE, JUICE.

This drink will make you more aware in a variety of different ways. You may want to dilute this with a little water since it's rather potent.

Calories: 421 kcal/ 1761 kj

Ingredients

- 6 kale leaves
- One whole broccoli head
- 1 cup spinach
- 2 green bell peppers
- 4 carrots

Instruction

In a juicer, first process the kale, broccoli, and spinach, and then go on to the carrots and bell peppers. Combine everything by giving it a thorough stir.

75. JUICE MADE FROM PUMPKIN

In addition to the health benefits, this is an excellent method for imparting the warm and cozy flavor of autumn into your beverage of choice. You may like the flavor of this juice even more if you add some cinnamon to it.

Calories: 427 kcal/ 1786 kj

Ingredients

- 6 carrots
- 2 sweet potatoes
- 2 squash

Instruction

In a juicer, begin by juicing the carrots and sweet potatoes, then go on to the squash and pumpkin. Combine everything by giving it a thorough stir.

76. SWEET POTATO PIE

This delightful drink also happens to be very good for you. It truly does taste like sweet potato pie! If you like the thing it is named after, you will most likely like this.
Calories: 468 kcal/ 1958 kj

Ingredients

- 4 sweet potatoes
- 4 carrots
- One-half of a teaspoon of cinnamon powder
- one-fourth of a teaspoon of ground cloves

Instruction

Use a juicer to make juice out of the carrots and sweet potatoes. After adding the cinnamon and cloves to the juice, thoroughly blend the ingredients by stirring them together.

77. VEGGIE BOOST

This juice is wonderful for treating a wide variety of illnesses. If you'd like more spiciness, add some black pepper or perhaps a jalapeño.
Calories: 443 kcal/ 1853 kj

Ingredients

- 2 cups spinach
- 3 basil leaves
- 6 Brussels sprouts
- 1 fennel bulb
- 1 cucumber

Instruction

The fennel and the cucumber should be juiced after the spinach, basil, and Brussels sprouts have been processed in the juicer. Combine everything by giving it a thorough stir.

78. SEEING GREEN

This one is quite straightforward: it is healthy for your eyes and green.
Calories: 288 kcal/ 1204 kj

Ingredients

- 2 cups spinach
- One whole broccoli head
- 1 cucumber

Instruction

In a juicer, first process the spinach and broccoli, and then go on to the cucumber. Combine everything by giving it a thorough stir.

79. THE PLEASURE OF APRICOTS

A delicious and refreshing juice with a hint of sweetness that will give you a boost. You may also like this with some ginger added to it.
Calories: 201 kcal/ 841 kj

Ingredients

- 3 carrots
- 2 apricots
- 1 cup diced cantaloupe

Instruction

First, the carrots are put through the juicer, followed by the apricots and the cantaloupe. Combine everything by giving it a thorough stir.

80. GREEN POPEYE JUICE

This combination will help strengthen both your eyes and your body. If you prefer things spicy, feel free to add a jalapeno to the mix. It will give it a nice kick.

Calories: 296 kcal/ 1238 kj

Ingredients

- 2 cups spinach
- 3 green bell peppers
- Four stalks of celery
- 1 cucumber

Instruction

The first thing to go through the juicer should be the spinach, followed by the bell peppers, celery, and cucumber. Combine everything by giving it a thorough stir.

81. PUNCH WITH PINEAPPLE AND CHERRIES

Use this fruity cocktail to flush out harmful free radicals. If you wish to serve this while entertaining guests, a splash of seltzer is the perfect accompaniment.
Calories: 294 kcal/ 1230 kj

Ingredients

- ¼ pineapple
- 2 plums
- 1 cup sour cherries

Instruction

Run all of the ingredients through a juicer, and then swirl the mixture very well to incorporate everything.

82. JULEP WITH CHERRY, BERRY, AND MINT

The addition of mint gives this sweet beverage an exciting dimension.
Calories: 406 kcal/ 1699 kj

Ingredients

- four sprigs of mint
- one cup of cherries
- one cup of raspberries
- one apple
- one cucumber

Instruction

In a juicer, first process the mint, then the cherries and raspberries, and last the cucumber and apple. Combine everything by giving it a thorough stir.

83. APPLE JUICE WITH MINT

This juice has a peculiar appearance when made, but it has a remarkable taste and is highly beneficial to your health.

Calories: 435 kcal/ 1820 kj

Ingredients

- 2 apples
- 1 carrot
- 1 pear
- 2 kiwis
- 4 sprigs of mint

Instruction

First, the mint is processed in the juicer, followed by the apples, carrots, and pears, and finally, the kiwis. Combine everything by giving it a thorough stir.

84. POTATO PINEAPPLE SPLASH

Ginger is a potent anti-inflammatory, and kiwis protect your heart and DNA from damage. When you combine all of these factors, you have a formula for living a long and healthy life.
Calories: 300 kcal/ 1255 kj

Ingredients

- One red potato
- Two kiwis
- One-fourth of a pineapple
- One-fourth of ginger

Instruction

In a juicer, first process the potato and ginger, then the kiwis, and last the pineapple. Combine everything by giving it a thorough stir.

85. JUICE MADE FROM POMEGRANATES AND CHERRIES

This drink is loaded with anti-inflammatory ingredients, which may help relieve the pain of arthritis. Cranberries are an excellent stand-in for pomegranates if you cannot locate them.
Calories: 379 kcal/ 1586 kj

Ingredients

- Two beets
- One-half cup of blackberries
- One pomegranate (or one cup of cranberries as an alternative)
- One-half cup of sour cherries
- Two kiwis

Instruction

Begin by putting the blackberries and beets through a juicer, and then go on to the pomegranate, cherries, and kiwis. Combine everything by giving it a thorough stir.

86. SIMPLY ORANGE

A really simple recipe, but certain things are ideal in their unaltered state!
Calories: 300 kcal/ 1255 kj

Ingredients

- Three complete oranges

Instruction

Put the oranges through a juicer to process them.

87. SPARKLING CITRUS FRUIT

This beverage is likely to improve both your state of mind and your immune system if you've been facing a severe sickness.
Calories: 274 kcal/ 1146 kj

Ingredients

- Two ounces of seltzer water
- One orange
- One lemon
- One-fourth of a pineapple

Instruction

Using a juicer, first process the pineapple, orange, and lemon, and then add the seltzer to the juice that is produced. To blend, give it a good stir.

88. NOT TO BE KISSED BUT HEALED

Following consumption of this beverage, your breath may not be very appealing to others (and hence, it might not be the ideal option to bring it to work). Still, your body will undoubtedly be grateful for the benefits it provides.

Calories: 347 kcal/ 1452 kj

Ingredients

- One cup of spinach
- One jalapeno pepper
- One onion
- Four carrots
- Two green bell peppers
- Two cloves of garlic
- One cucumber

Instruction

A juicer should be used to process the spinach, onion, and jalapeno first, followed by the carrots, bell peppers, garlic, and finally the cucumber. To blend, give it a good stir.

89. GESUNDHEIT GAZPACHO

This refreshing juice will end your runny nose if you drink it.
Calories: 147 kcal/ 615 kj

Ingredients

- 2 tomatoes
- 1 green bell pepper
- 2 green onions
- 1 garlic clove

Instruction

Run all of the ingredients through a juicer, and then swirl the mixture very well to incorporate everything.

90. MUSCLE ACHE DRINK

The combination of these ingredients is ideal for providing a post-workout surge of energy or for providing an immunity enhancement if you are feeling run down.
Calories: 434 kcal/ 1816 kj

Ingredients

- One apple
- Four Carrots
- One Head of Broccoli
- One Cup of Spinach
- Six Leaves of Kale

Instruction

Utilizing the juicer, first process the spinach and kale, then the broccoli and carrots, and finish with the apple. To blend, give it a good stir.

91. GINGER JUICE

Is great for hydrating you and calming an upset stomach when you have the flu, but it also helps settle an upset stomach.
Calories: 27 kcal/ 113 kj

Ingredients

- 4 cups of water
- a piece of ginger about 2 inches
- a quarter of a lemon

Instruction

After the water has come to a boil, put the ginger into it. Bring to a boil, then simmer for fifteen to twenty minutes. The ginger should be discarded once the tea has been strained. Squeeze in lemon juice to taste.

92. GINGER APPLE FIZZ

"An apple a day" and some ginger make this a terrific cold-prevention juice, and you can have both ingredients in this fizzy drink.

Calories: 308 kcal/ 1289 kj

Ingredients

- One pear
- Two apples
- Two ounces of seltzer water
- A half-inch slice of ginger

Instruction

First, the ginger is put through the juicer, followed by the pears and apples. After adding the seltzer to the juice, give the mixture a good toss to integrate the two.

93. GREEN CARROT

If you want to dilute the intensity of this juice a little bit, you may try adding a quarter cup of water. It becomes even better to throw in a jalapeno pepper to spice things up.
Calories: 625 kcal/ 2615 kj

Ingredients

- 2 cups of spinach
- 1 head of broccoli
- 6 carrots
- 2 cups of Brussels sprouts

Instruction

The carrots should be juiced first, followed by spinach, Brussels sprouts, and broccoli in the food processor. To blend, give it a good stir.

94. GREEN APPLE GRAPE

This delicious and mellow juice combination has been around for decades. It is important to remember that certain stringent juicing fasts do not allow the use of honeydew since the pulp might seep through.

Calories: 425 kcal/ 1778 kj

Ingredients

- 2 green apples
- 1 cup of diced honeydew melon
- 1 cup of red grapes

Instruction

In a juicer, first process the apples and grapes, and then go on to the honeydew. To blend, give it a good stir.

95. GRANNY'S GO JUICE HAS ARRIVED!

The ideal way to enjoy this juice is either as a sweet treat or with your breakfast because of its high sugar content. However, it does have a very high antioxidant content and many positive effects on one's health, so you shouldn't feel too bad about indulging in it.

Calories: 363 kcal/ 1519 kj

Ingredients

- 2 cups of wheatgrass
- Three carrots
- One beet
- One cup each of strawberries and blueberries
- One teaspoon of powdered cinnamon

Instruction

In a juicer, begin by juicing the wheatgrass, then go on to the carrots and beet, and finish with the berries, strawberries, and blueberries. After adding the cinnamon to the juice, give it a good toss to blend the two ingredients.

96. THE INCREDIBLE POPEYE

This is a juice with a robust flavor that may not be to everyone's taste, but it is simply outstanding in terms of how well it promotes health and slows the aging process.
Calories: 453 kcal/ 1895 kj

Ingredients

- 2 cups of spinach
- 1 head of broccoli
- 1 artichoke
- 4 carrots
- 1 cucumber

Instruction

Using a juicer, first process the spinach and broccoli, and then go on to the artichoke, carrots, and cucumber. To blend, give it a good stir.

97. VEGGIE DELIGHT

This flavor is similar to a spicy Bloody Mary mix but with a little more bite. When you process the tomato last, you'll help force more liquid and nutrients from the other components into your juice. This will help you get more juice out of your ingredients.

Calories: 156 kcal/ 653 kj

Ingredients

- 4 sprigs of basil
- 3 carrots
- 1 teaspoon of grated horseradish
- 1 tomato
- 1 green bell pepper
- 1/4 teaspoon of cayenne pepper

Instruction

In a juicer, begin by processing the basil and carrots, then go on to the horseradish and bell pepper, and finish with the tomato. After adding the cayenne to the juice, give it a good toss to blend the two ingredients.

98. JUICE FOR ENDLESS YOUTH AND BEAUTY

By preparing this drink regularly, you may keep yourself looking and feeling younger for longer. This juice has a more refreshing taste because of the addition of the cucumber.
Calories: 393 kcal/ 1644 kj

Ingredients

- Two cups of spinach
- Half a head of broccoli
- One-half of a sweet potato
- Three carrots
- One bulb of garlic
- One cucumber

Instruction

A juicer should first be used to process the spinach, broccoli, and sweet potato, followed by the carrots, garlic, and cucumber. To blend, give it a good stir.

99. FINE LINE WINE

This dish, loaded with berries, is an excellent option for breakfast. Get a potent dose of antioxidants to start your day!
Calories: 407 kcal/ 1703 kj

Ingredients

• 2 apples
• 1/2 cup each of the following berries: blueberries, blackberries, raspberries, strawberries, and red grapes

Instruction

Run all of the ingredients through a juicer, and then swirl the mixture very well to incorporate everything.

100.   ANTIOXIDANT PUNCH

Weighty benefits include protection against cancer and the appearance of wrinkles.
Calories: 163 kcal/ 682 kj

Ingredients

- 2 stalks of celery
- 1 cucumber
- 1 cup of blueberries

Instruction

First, the celery is put through the juicer, followed by the cucumber and the blueberries. To blend, give it a good stir.

Conclusion

The medical profession is divided on the efficacy of juice cleanses since, contrary to popular belief, these diets often do not lead to sustainable weight reduction or improvements in overall health. Instead, the majority of health professionals will advise following a diet that is both balanced and healthy.

The data that may support the potential advantages of juicing is often anecdotal. More data is demonstrating that juice cleanses might have a harmful influence on the body, such as by lowering the function of the kidneys.

We hope that the information presented here will assist you in making better-educated decisions about juicing these three veggies, whether you choose to juice them separately or use them as components of juicing recipe combinations.

We believe it is just as vital to commit to making better choices about nutrition and lifestyle, which will eventually affect one's long-term health, as it is to drink juice regularly as part of a health-enhancing regimen.

Because juicing might cause residues of chemicals to be left behind, it is important to use only organic fruits and vegetables rather than those produced using traditional farming methods if you want to make your juice.

People should consult their primary care physicians before beginning a juice cleanse to see whether they need to adjust their current juicing regimen to maintain or improve their overall state of health.

BASIC CONVERSION CHARTS

weight
(rounded to the nearest whole number)

IMPERIAL	METRIC
0.5 oz	14 g
1 oz	28 g
2 oz	58 g
3 oz	86 g
4 oz	114 g
5 oz	142 g
6 oz	170 g
7 oz	198 g
8 oz (1/2 lb)	226 g
9 oz	256 g
10 oz	284 g
11 oz	312 g
12 oz	340 g
13 oz	368 g
14 oz	396 g
15 oz	426 g
16 oz (1 lb)	454 g
24 oz (1 1/2 lb)	680 g

misc
(rounded to the closest equivalent)

IMPERIAL	
1 quart	4 cups (1 liter)
4 quarts	16 cups (4.5 liters)
6 quarts	24 cups (7 liters)
1 gallon	16 cups (4.5 liters)

volume
(rounded to the closest equivalent)

IMPERIAL	METRIC
1/8 tsp	0.5 mL
1/4 tsp	1 mL
1/2 tsp	2.5 mL
3/4 tsp	4 mL
1 tsp	5 mL
1 tbsp	15 mL
1 1/2 tbsp	25 mL
1/8 cup	30 mL
1/4 cup	60 mL
1/3 cup	80 mL
1/2 cup	120 mL
2/3 cup	160 mL
3/4 cup	180 mL
1 cup	240 mL

liquid
(rounded to the closest equivalent)

IMPERIAL	METRIC
0.5 oz	15 mL
1 oz	30 mL
2 oz	60 mL
3 oz	85 mL
4 oz	115 mL
5 oz	140 mL
6 oz	170 mL
7 oz	200 mL
8 oz	230 mL
9 oz	260 mL
10 oz	285 mL
11 oz	310 mL
12 oz	340 mL
13 oz	370 mL

temperature
(rounded to the closest equivalent)

IMPERIAL	METRIC
150°F	65°C
160°F	70°C
175°F	80°C
200°F	95°C
225°F	110°C
250°F	120°C
275°F	135°C
300°F	150°C
325°F	160°C
350°F	175°C
375°F	190°C
400°F	205°C
425°F	220°C
450°F	230°C
475°F	245°C
500°F	260°C

length
(rounded to the closest equivalent)

IMPERIAL	METRIC
1/8 inch	3 mm
1/4 inch	6 mm
1 inch	2.5 cm
1 1/4 inch	3 cm
2 inches	5 cm
6 inches	15 cm
8 inches	20 cm
9 inches	22.5 cm
10 inches	25 cm
11 inches	28 cm

COOKING MEASUREMENT CONVERSION CHART

QUICK ALTERNATIVES

1	tablespoon (tbsp)	3 teaspoons (tsp)
1/16	cup	1 tablespoon
1/8	cup	2 tablespoons
1/6	cup	2 tablespoons + 2 teaspoons
1/4	cup	4 tablespoons
1/3	cup	5 tablespoons + 1 teaspoon
3/8	cup	6 tablespoons
1/2	cup	8 tablespoons
2/3	cup	10 tablespoons + 2 teaspoons
3/4	cup	12 tablespoons
1	cup	48 teaspoons
1	cup	16 tablespoons
8	fluid ounces (fl oz)	1 cup
1	pint (pt)	2 cups
1	quart (qt)	2 pints
4	cups	1 quart
1	gallon (gal)	4 quarts
16	ounces (oz)	1 pound (lb)
1	milliliter (ml)	1 cubic centimeter (cc)
1	inch (in)	2.54 centimeters (cm)

CAPACITY (U.S to Metric)

1/5 teaspoon	1 milliliter
1 teaspoon	5 ml
1 tablespoon	15 ml
1 fluid oz	30 ml
1/5 cup	47 ml
1 cup	237 ml
2 cups (1 pint)	473 ml
4 cups (1 quart)	.95 liter
4 quarts (1 gal.)	3.8 liters

WEIGHT (U.S to Metric)

1	oz	28 grams
1	pound	454 grams

CAPACITY (Metric to U.S.)

1	milliliter	1/5 teaspoon
5	ml	1 teaspoon
15	ml	1 tablespoon
100	ml	3.4 fluid oz
240	ml	1 cup
		34 fluid oz
		4.2 cups
1	liter	2.1 pints
		1.06 quarts
		0.26 gallon

WEIGHT (Metric to U.S.)

1	gram	0.035 ounce
100	grams	3.5 ounces
500	grams	1.1 pounds
1	kilogram	2.205 pounds
		35 ounces

Printed in Great Britain
by Amazon

20818666R00068